# THIS BOOK

# BELONGS TO

_____

_____

_____

## A Message to the Fabulous Teachers of the World

A teacher's to-do list is usually longer than the number of hours in a day. The overwhelming scope of work demands easily create stress and anxiety. This is exacerbated on Sunday nights. Sunday nights create stress and anxiety in anticipation of the upcoming workweek. It's impossible for teachers to avoid lesson planning and preparing for the week but with strategic planning, teachers can alleviate some of the stress by using some time for reflection and relaxation. Reflective teachers uses self-assessment to identify their strengths and weaknesses and proactively develop a plan of action for future success.

## How to Use This Book

When the weekend quickly escapes you and Sunday night anxiety begins to creep up, grab a nice cup of tea or a glass of wine and color one of the pages. Your favorite music enhances the experience even more. (I prefer smooth jazz.) Next, use this calm and relaxed energy to complete the reflection sheet. It will help you relinquish some of the anxiety and leave you feeling prepared to tackle your upcoming week. Don't forget to use the weekly affirmation to guide your steps. Color! Relax! Release!

Thank you for your patronage. Please leave an honest review. My ability to create quality books depends on it. Feedback helps me make necessary improvements.

If you would like complimentary coloring pages not found in this book, please feel free to email me at Chanel2104@gmail.com

# *Weekly Reflection*

Date _____/_____/_____

| | |
|---|---|
| **Greatest Accomplishments** | |
| **My Biggest Impact** | |
| **Areas to Improve** | |
| **Next Steps** | |

*Weekly Affirmation*: *The work I do matters.*

# Notes

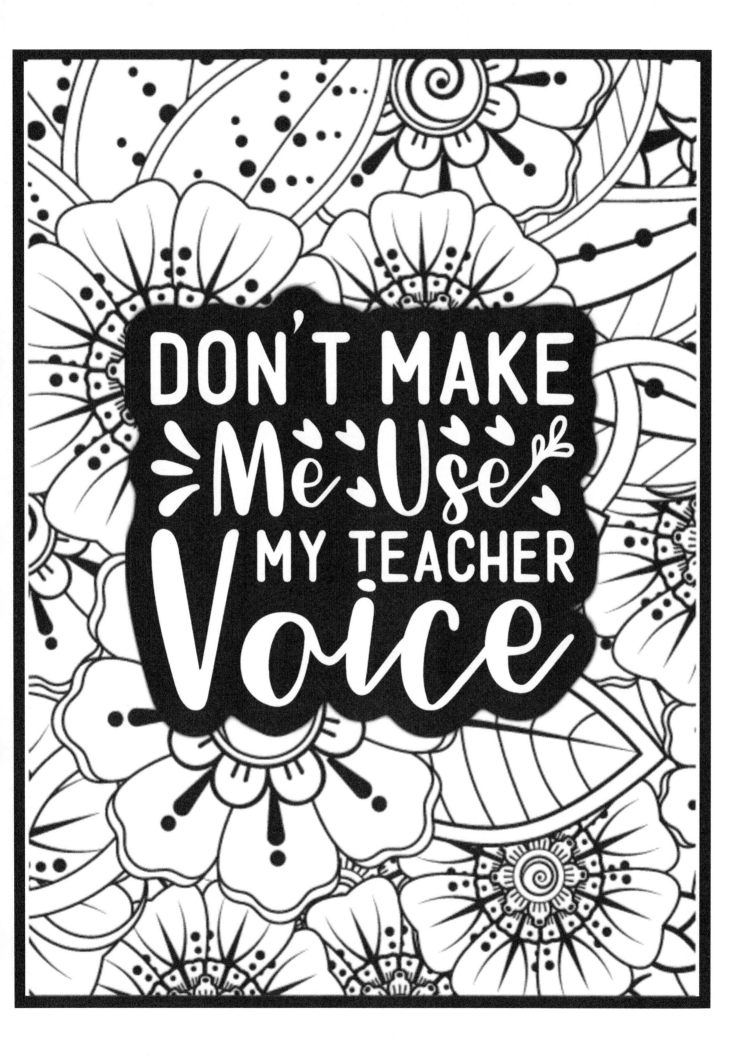

# Weekly Reflection

Date _____/_____/_____

| | |
|---|---|
| Greatest Accomplishments | |
| My Biggest Impact | |
| Areas to Improve | |
| Next Steps | |

*Weekly Affirmation: My classroom is a place where children feel valued.*

# Notes

# Weekly Reflection

Date _____/_____/_____

| | |
|---|---|
| **Greatest Accomplishments** | |
| **My Biggest Impact** | |
| **Areas to Improve** | |
| **Next Steps** | |

*Weekly Affirmation:* I strive for progress, not perfection.

# Notes

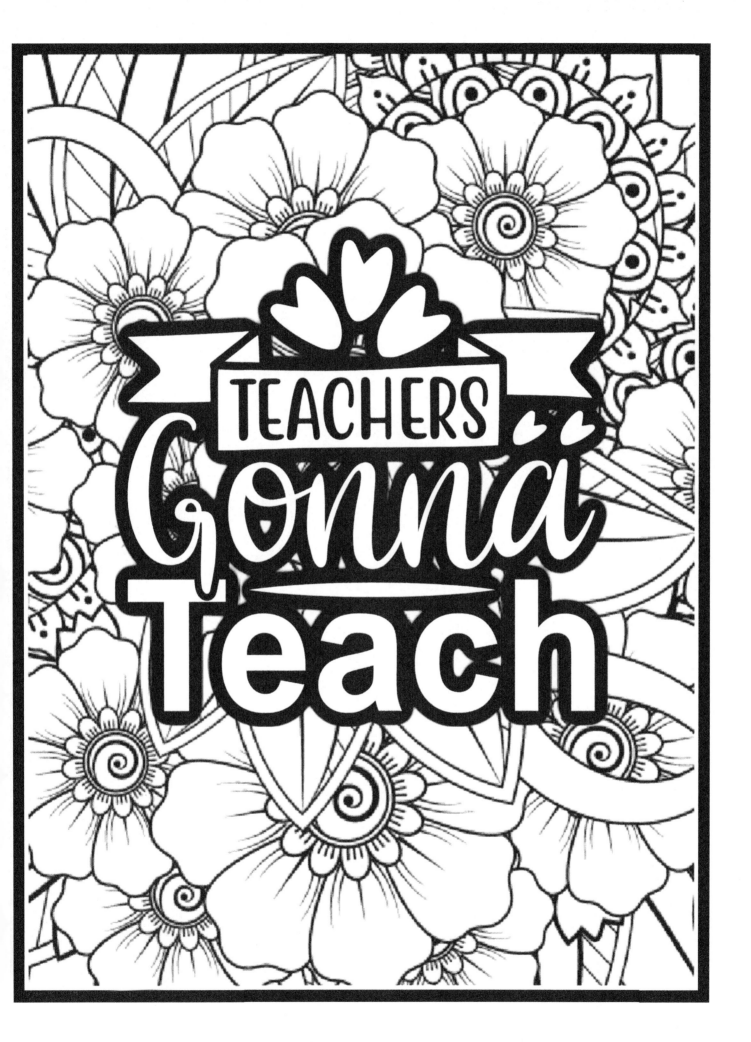

# Weekly Reflection

Date _____/_____/_____

| | |
|---|---|
| **Greatest Accomplishments** | |
| **My Biggest Impact** | |
| **Areas to Improve** | |
| **Next Steps** | |

*Weekly Affirmation*: *Setbacks are setups for comebacks.*

# Notes

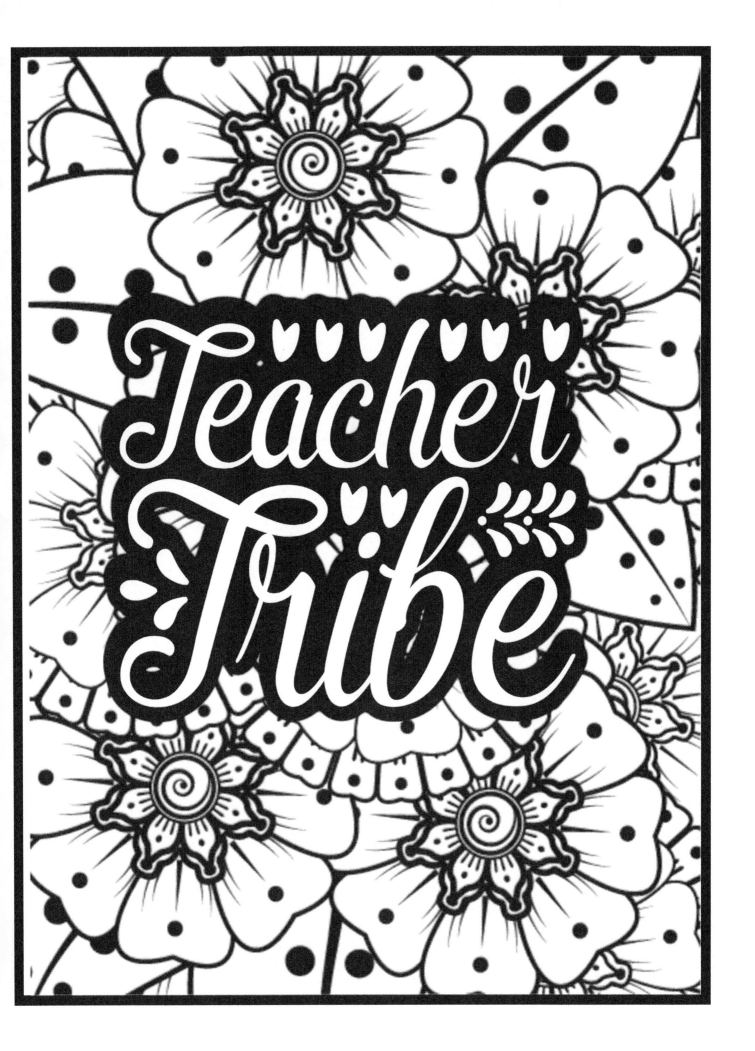

# Weekly Reflection

Date _____/_____/_____

| | |
|---|---|
| Greatest Accomplishments | |
| My Biggest Impact | |
| Areas to Improve | |
| Next Steps | |

*Weekly Affirmation*: *I'm brave enough to attempt.*

# Notes

# *Weekly Reflection*

Date _____/_____/_____

| | |
|---|---|
| **Greatest Accomplishments** | |
| **My Biggest Impact** | |
| **Areas to Improve** | |
| **Next Steps** | |

*Weekly Affirmation:* I am capable of doing difficult things.

# Notes

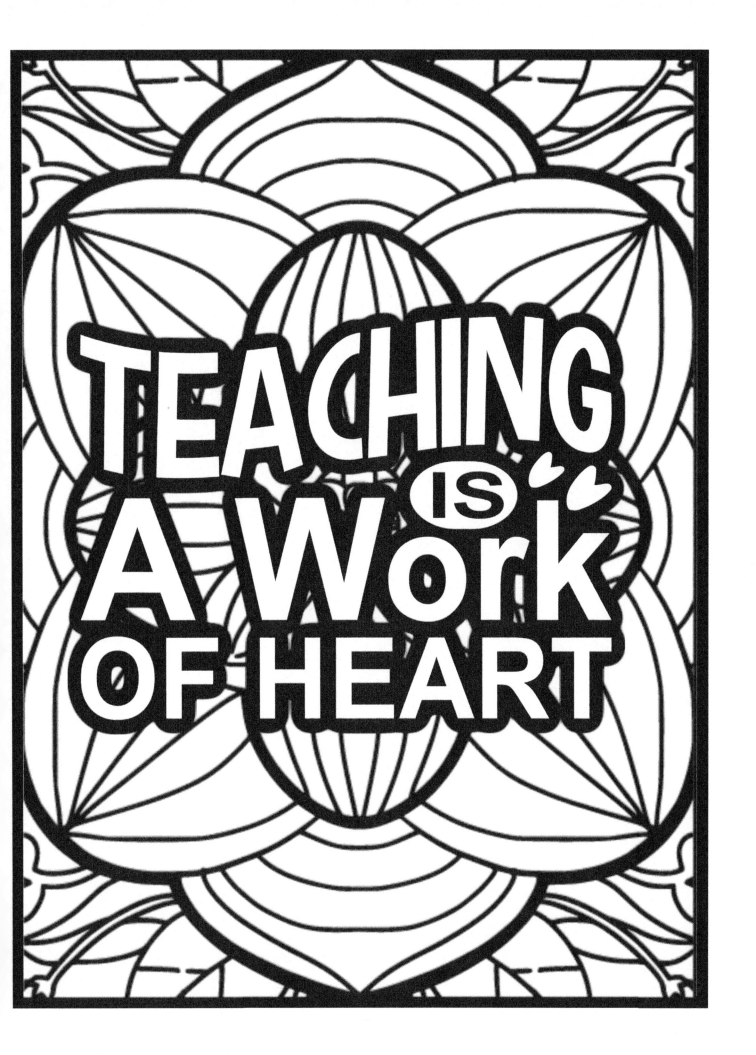

# Weekly Reflection

Date _____ / _____ / _____

| | |
|---|---|
| **Greatest Accomplishments** | |
| **My Biggest Impact** | |
| **Areas to Improve** | |
| **Next Steps** | |

*Weekly Affirmation:* *I do my best and that is enough.*

# Notes

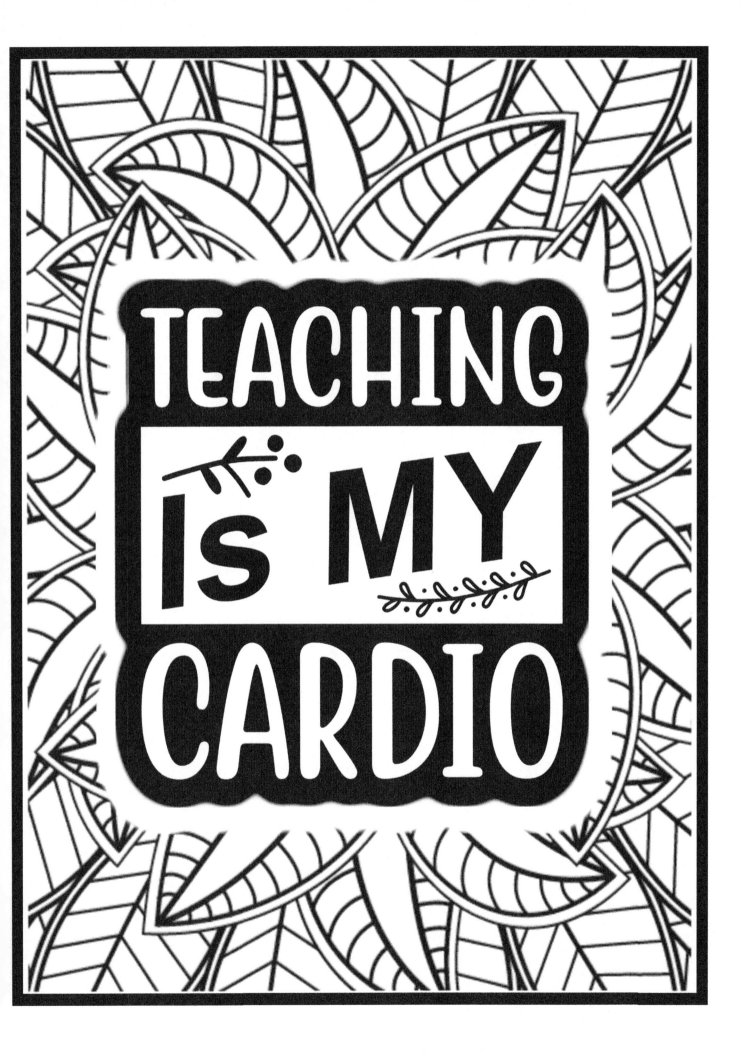

# Weekly Reflection

Date \_\_\_\_\_/\_\_\_\_\_/\_\_\_\_\_

| | |
|---|---|
| **Greatest Accomplishments** | |
| **My Biggest Impact** | |
| **Areas to Improve** | |
| **Next Steps** | |

*Weekly Affirmation*: *My classroom is a safe space for growing and learning.*

# Notes

# Weekly Reflection

Date _____/_____/_____

| | |
|---|---|
| Greatest Accomplishments | |
| My Biggest Impact | |
| Areas to Improve | |
| Next Steps | |

*Weekly Affirmation:* I can and I will!

# Notes

# Weekly Reflection

Date _____/_____/_____

| | |
|---|---|
| Greatest Accomplishments | |
| My Biggest Impact | |
| Areas to Improve | |
| Next Steps | |

*Weekly Affirmation: I embody an attitude of gratitude.*

# Notes

# Weekly Reflection

Date _____/_____/_____

| | |
|---|---|
| Greatest Accomplishments | |
| My Biggest Impact | |
| Areas to Improve | |
| Next Steps | |

*Weekly Affirmation*: *I manifest successful outcomes.*

# Notes

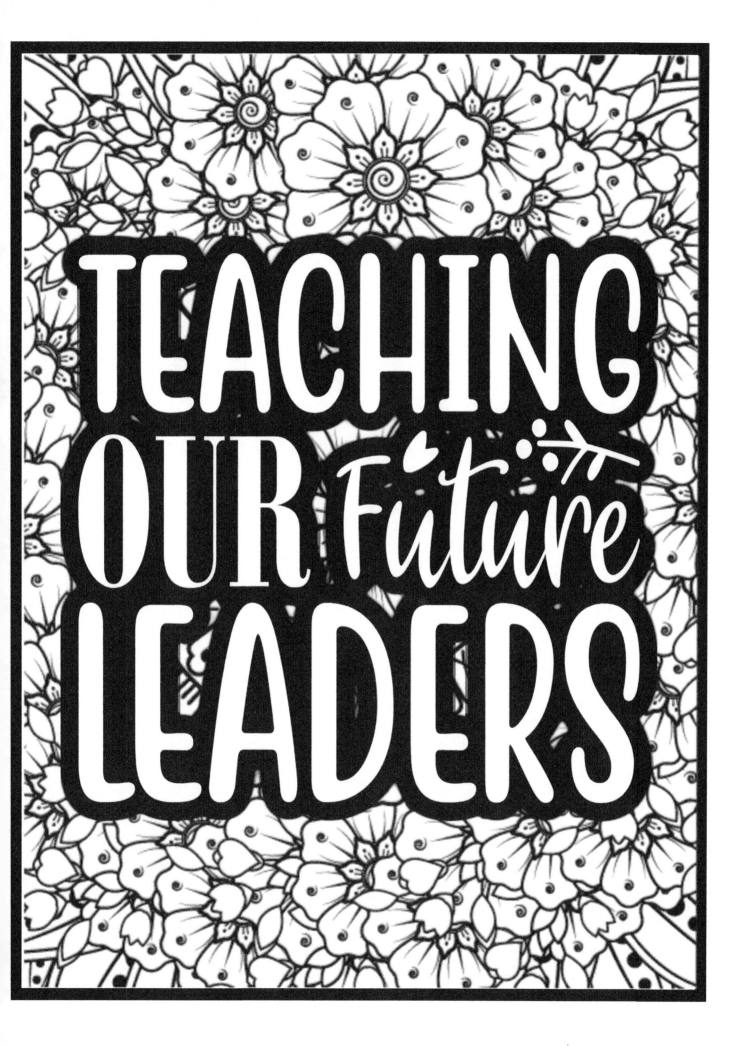

# Weekly Reflection

Date _____/_____/_____

| | |
|---|---|
| **Greatest Accomplishments** | |
| **My Biggest Impact** | |
| **Areas to Improve** | |
| **Next Steps** | |

*Weekly Affirmation*: *I am worthy of the greatest things in life.*

# Notes

# Weekly Reflection

Date _____/_____/_____

| | |
|---|---|
| Greatest Accomplishments | |
| My Biggest Impact | |
| Areas to Improve | |
| Next Steps | |

*Weekly Affirmation:* My positive attitude is infectious to my students.

# Notes

# Weekly Reflection

Date _____/_____/_____

| | |
|---|---|
| **Greatest Accomplishments** | |
| **My Biggest Impact** | |
| **Areas to Improve** | |
| **Next Steps** | |

*Weekly Affirmation:* I enhance the lives of future generations.

# Notes

# Weekly Reflection

Date _____/_____/_____

| | |
|---|---|
| Greatest Accomplishments | |
| My Biggest Impact | |
| Areas to Improve | |
| Next Steps | |

*Weekly Affirmation:* I embrace my whole self unconditionally.

# Notes

# Weekly Reflection

Date _____/_____/_____

| | |
|---|---|
| Greatest Accomplishments | |
| My Biggest Impact | |
| Areas to Improve | |
| Next Steps | |

*Weekly Affirmation*: *My growth comes through trial and error.*

# Notes

# Weekly Reflection

Date _____/_____/_____

| | |
|---|---|
| **Greatest Accomplishments** | |
| **My Biggest Impact** | |
| **Areas to Improve** | |
| **Next Steps** | |

*Weekly Affirmation: I am fearless and welcome challenges.*

# Notes

# Weekly Reflection

Date _____ / _____ / _____

| | |
|---|---|
| **Greatest Accomplishments** | |
| **My Biggest Impact** | |
| **Areas to Improve** | |
| **Next Steps** | |

*Weekly Affirmation*: *Taking on challenges is my superpower.*

# Notes

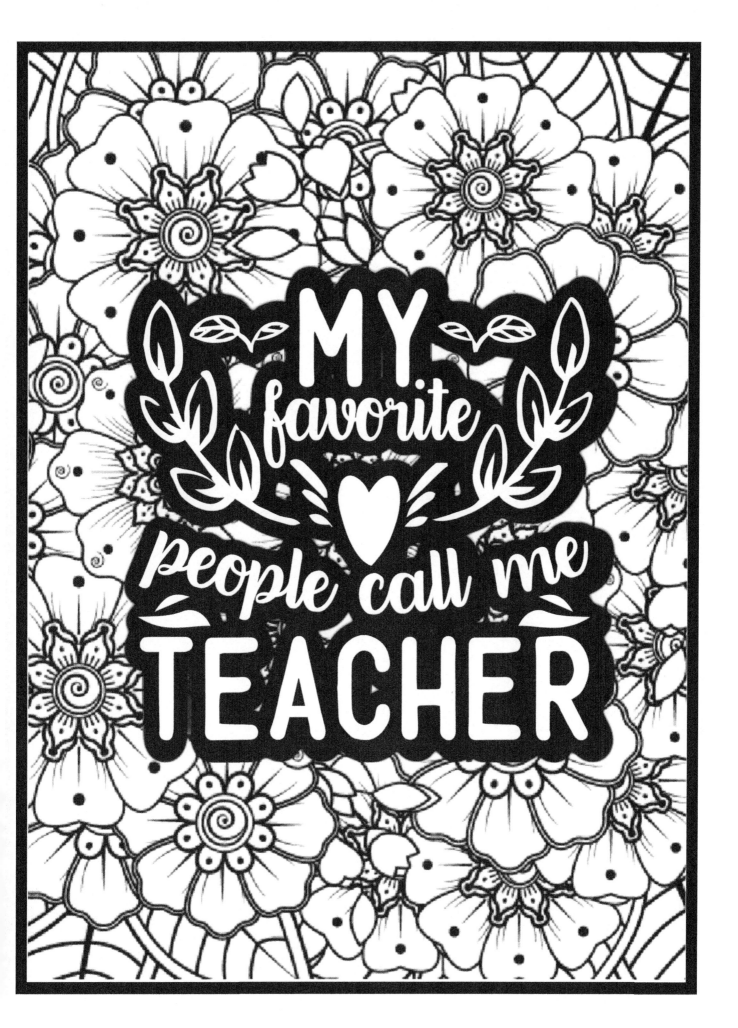

# Weekly Reflection

Date _____/_____/_____

| | |
|---|---|
| **Greatest Accomplishments** | |
| **My Biggest Impact** | |
| **Areas to Improve** | |
| **Next Steps** | |

*Weekly Affirmation:* My mishaps do not define me.

# Notes

# Weekly Reflection

Date _____/_____/_____

| | |
|---|---|
| Greatest Accomplishments | |
| My Biggest Impact | |
| Areas to Improve | |
| Next Steps | |

*Weekly Affirmation*: *I approach every day with gratitude and love.*

# Notes

# Weekly Reflection

Date _____ / _____ / _____

| | |
|---|---|
| **Greatest Accomplishments** | |
| **My Biggest Impact** | |
| **Areas to Improve** | |
| **Next Steps** | |

*Weekly Affirmation*: *Everything happens in its divine right time.*

# Notes

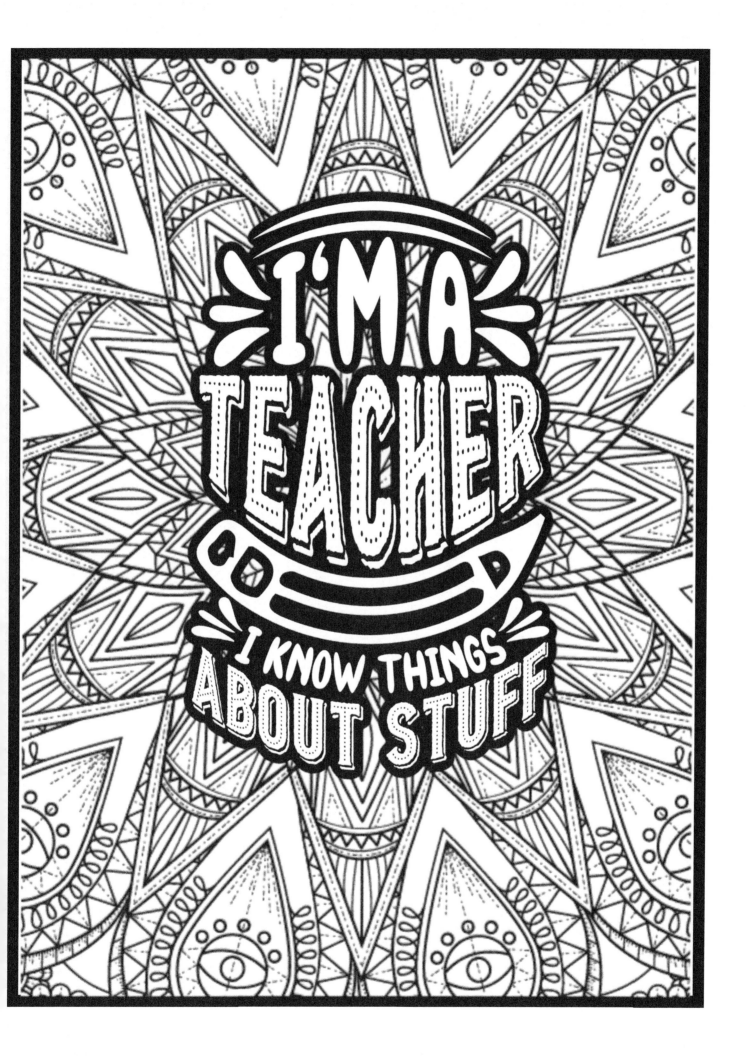

# Weekly Reflection

Date _____/_____/_____

| | |
|---|---|
| **Greatest Accomplishments** | |
| **My Biggest Impact** | |
| **Areas to Improve** | |
| **Next Steps** | |

*Weekly Affirmation: With this new day I welcome positive energy.*

# Notes

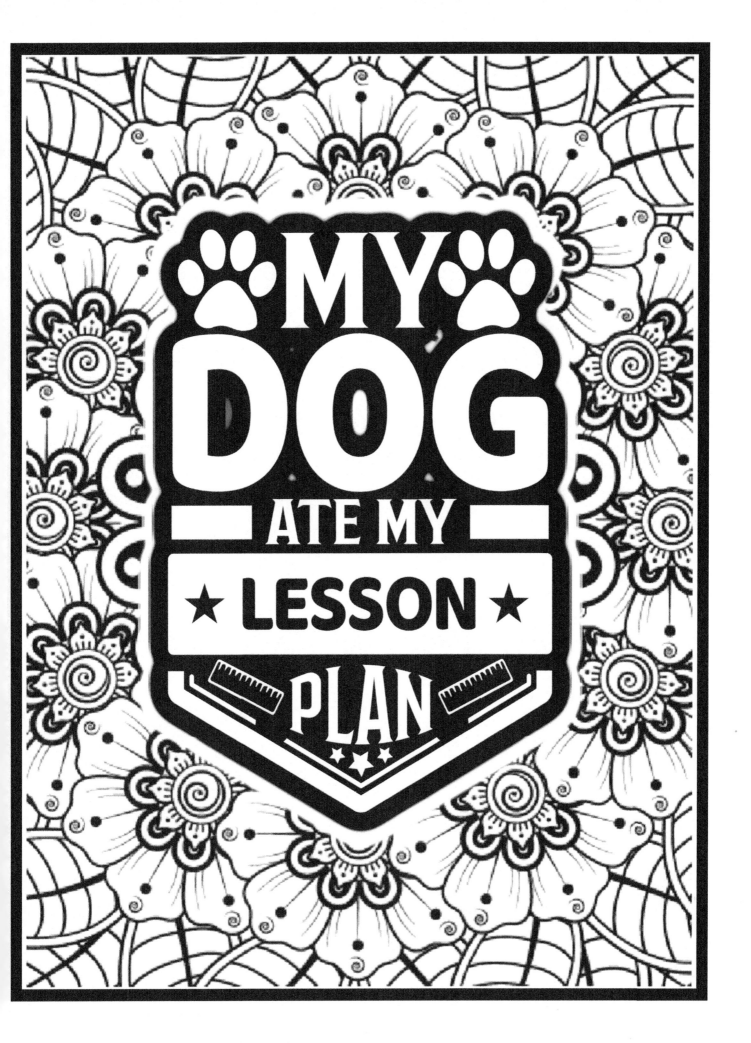

# Weekly Reflection

Date _____/_____/_____

| | |
|---|---|
| **Greatest Accomplishments** | |
| **My Biggest Impact** | |
| **Areas to Improve** | |
| **Next Steps** | |

*Weekly Affirmation:* I have the power to release my insecurities.

# Notes

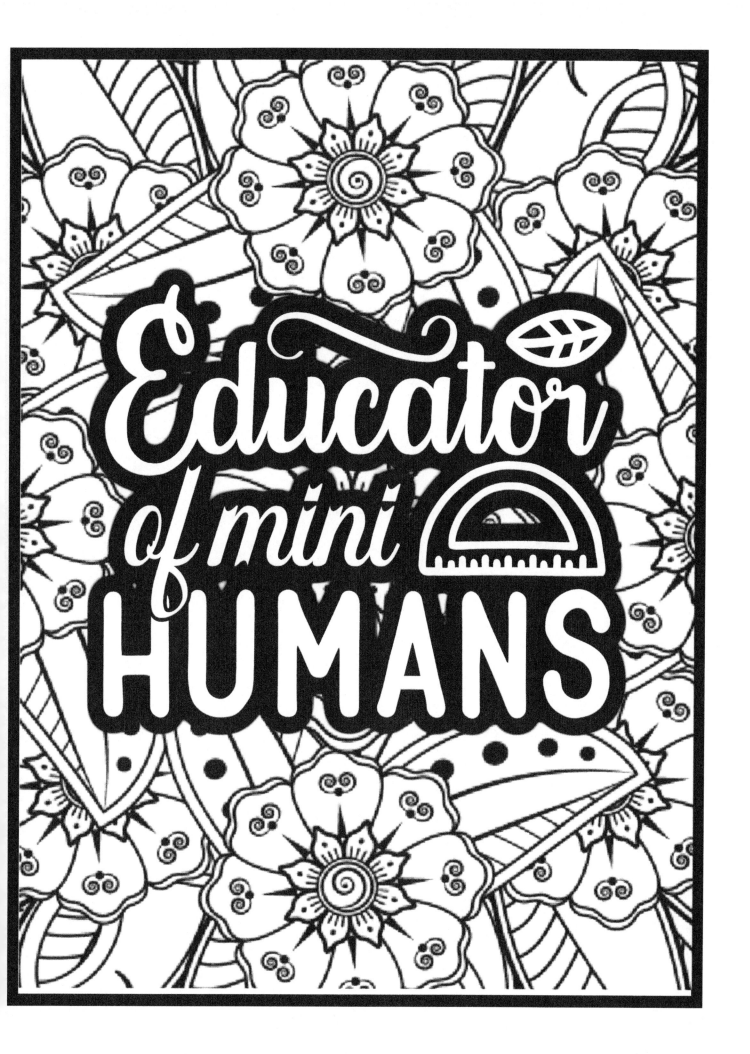

# Weekly Reflection

Date _____/_____/_____

| | |
|---|---|
| **Greatest Accomplishments** | |
| **My Biggest Impact** | |
| **Areas to Improve** | |
| **Next Steps** | |

*Weekly Affirmation: Self-doubt stands no chance against my inner strength.*

# Notes

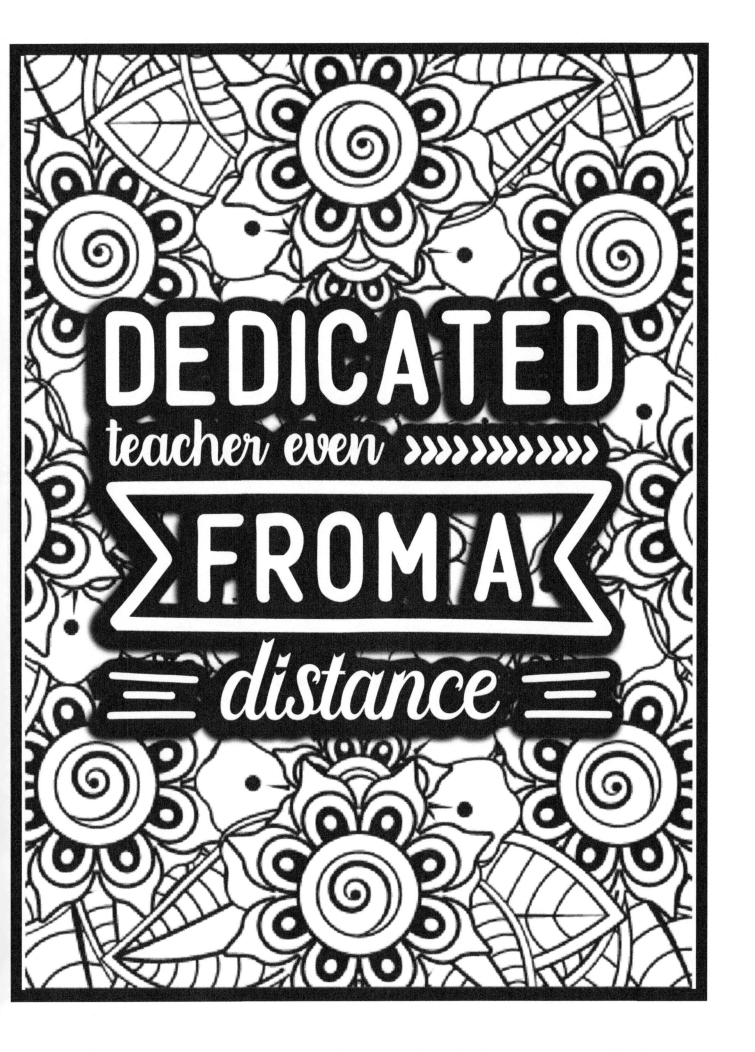

# Weekly Reflection

Date _____/_____/_____

| | |
|---|---|
| **Greatest Accomplishments** | |
| **My Biggest Impact** | |
| **Areas to Improve** | |
| **Next Steps** | |

*Weekly Affirmation*: *I choose to have the best day ever!*

# Notes

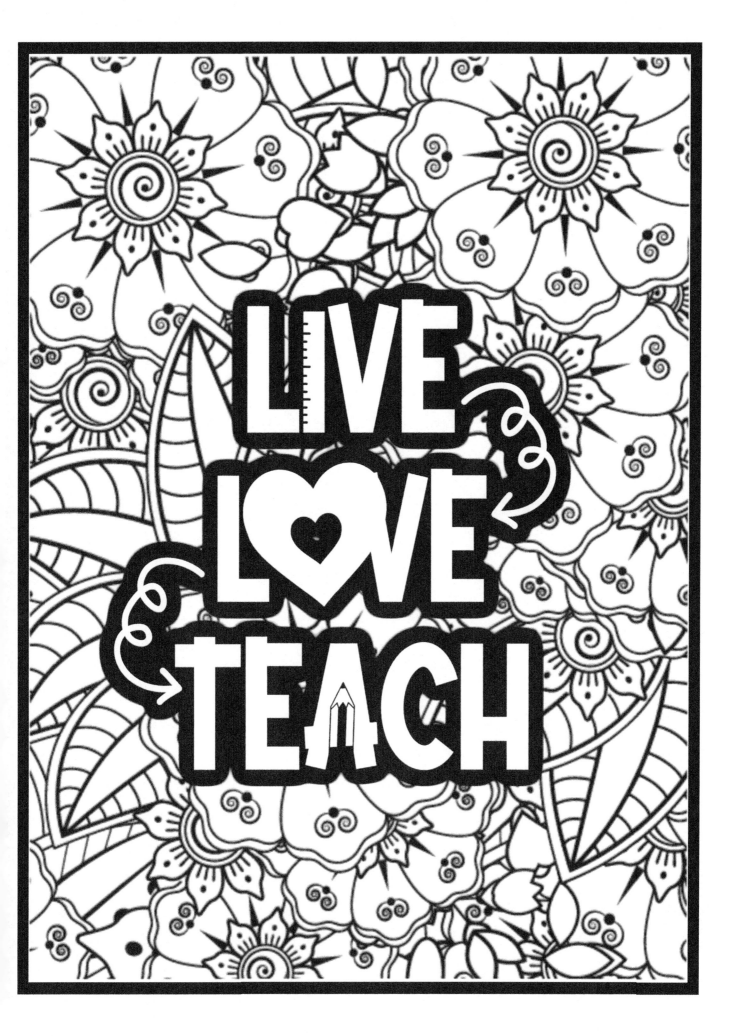

# Weekly Reflection

Date _____/_____/_____

| | |
|---|---|
| Greatest Accomplishments | |
| My Biggest Impact | |
| Areas to Improve | |
| Next Steps | |

*Weekly Affirmation: Unconditional love flows to and through me.*

# Notes

# Weekly Reflection

Date _____/_____/_____

| | |
|---|---|
| **Greatest Accomplishments** | |
| **My Biggest Impact** | |
| **Areas to Improve** | |
| **Next Steps** | |

*Weekly Affirmation:* I reserve the right to protect my emotional well-being.

# Notes

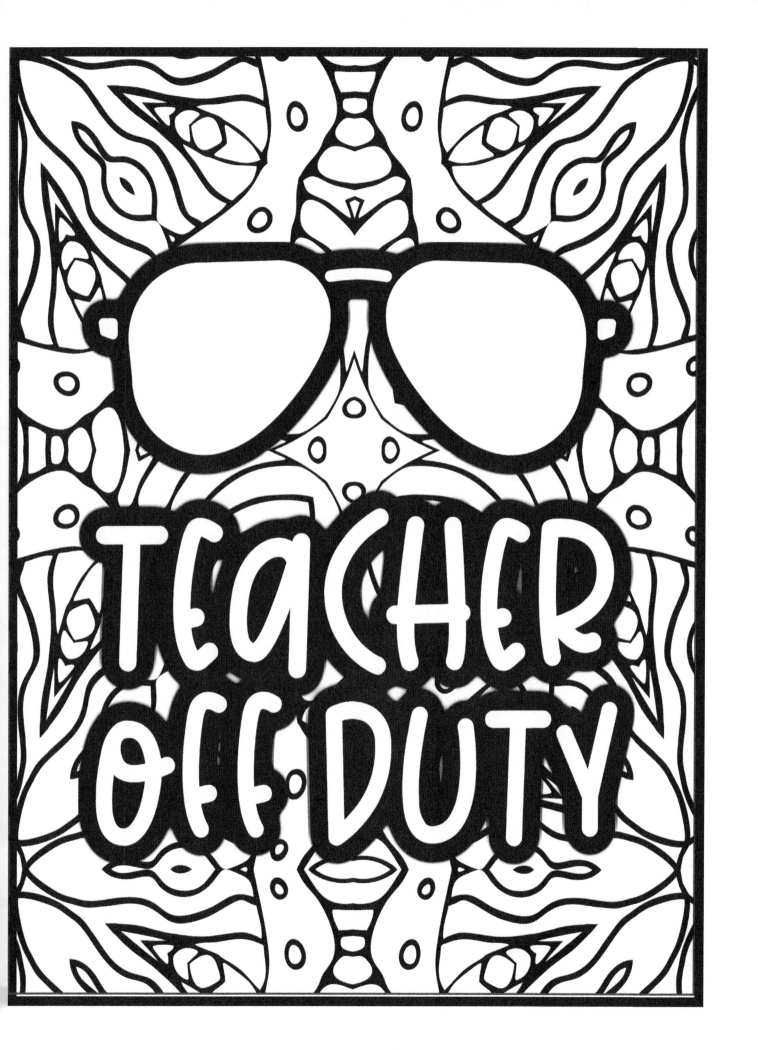

# Weekly Reflection

Date _____/_____/_____

| | |
|---|---|
| **Greatest Accomplishments** | |
| **My Biggest Impact** | |
| **Areas to Improve** | |
| **Next Steps** | |

*Weekly Affirmation*: *When I don't succeed right away, I try again.*

# Notes

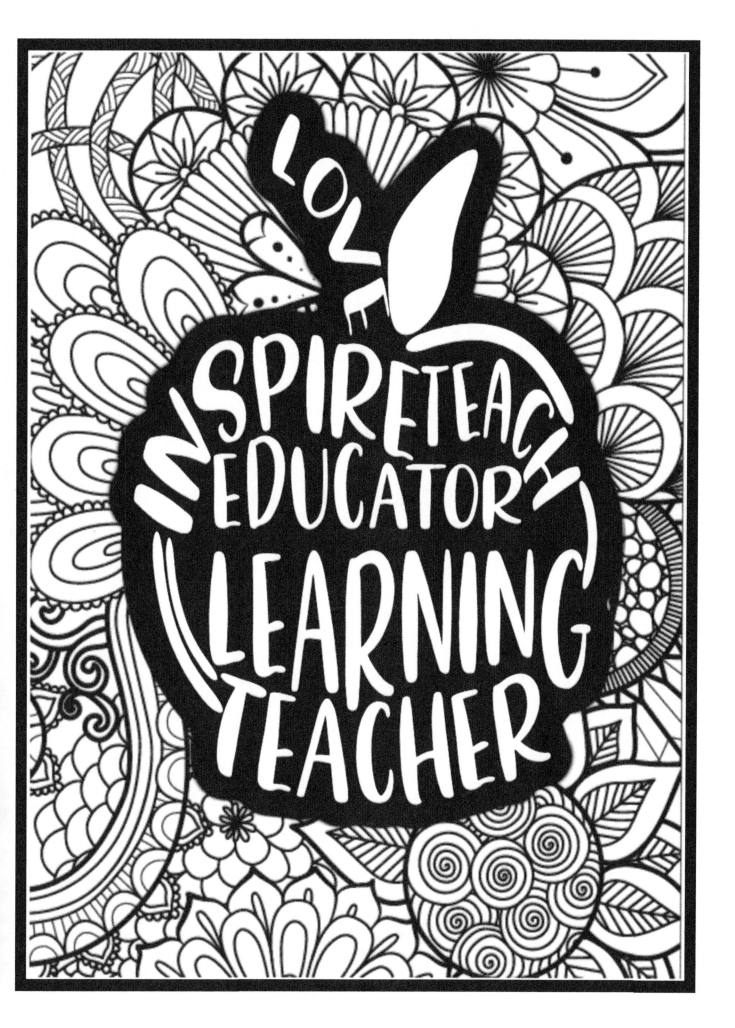

# Weekly Reflection

Date _____/_____/_____

| | |
|---|---|
| **Greatest Accomplishments** | |
| **My Biggest Impact** | |
| **Areas to Improve** | |
| **Next Steps** | |

*Weekly Affirmation*: *I trust my instincts and listen to my wise inner voice.*

# Notes

# Weekly Reflection

Date _____/_____/_____

| | |
|---|---|
| **Greatest Accomplishments** | |
| **My Biggest Impact** | |
| **Areas to Improve** | |
| **Next Steps** | |

*Weekly Affirmation: I forgive myself for my missteps and mistakes.*

# Notes

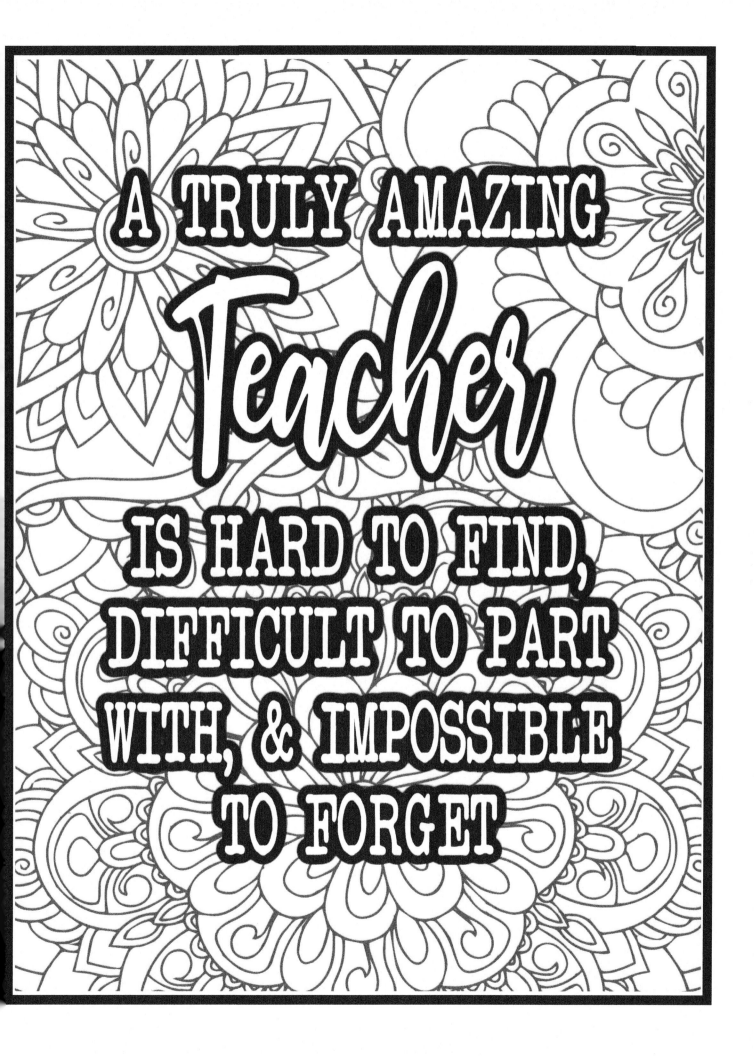

# Weekly Reflection

Date _____/_____/_____

| | |
|---|---|
| Greatest Accomplishments | |
| My Biggest Impact | |
| Areas to Improve | |
| Next Steps | |

*Weekly Affirmation:* I learn from my negative experiences.

# Notes

# Weekly Reflection

Date _____/_____/_____

| | |
|---|---|
| Greatest Accomplishments | |
| My Biggest Impact | |
| Areas to Improve | |
| Next Steps | |

*Weekly Affirmation:* I am the inspiration that I want to see!

# Notes

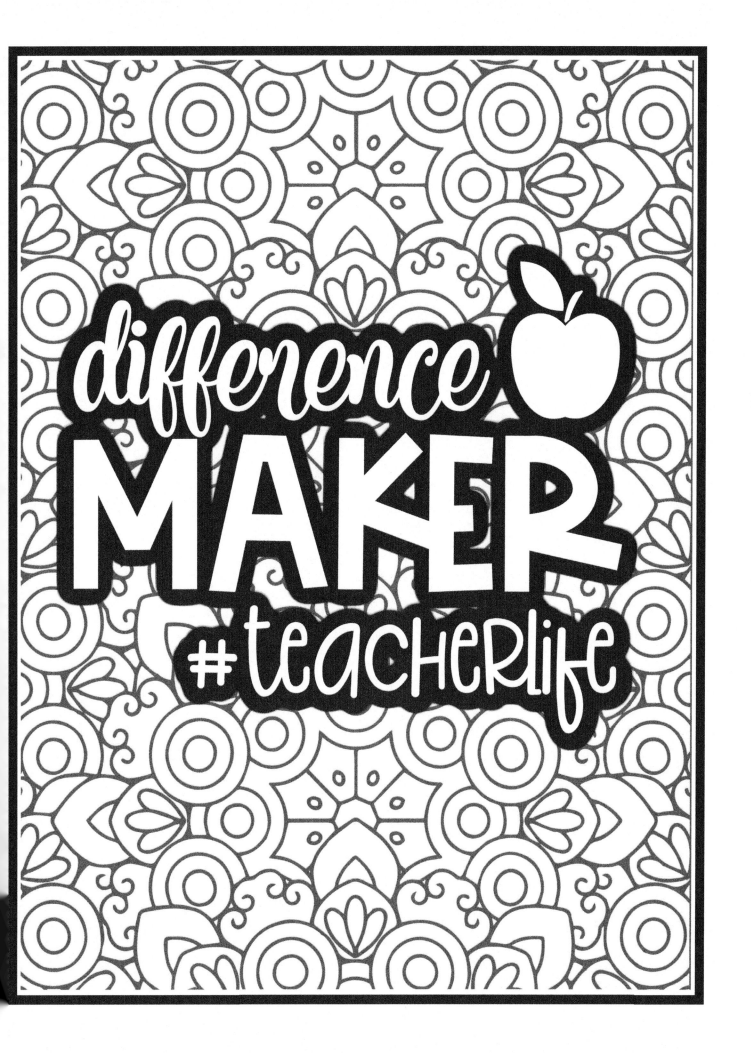

# Weekly Reflection

Date _____/_____/_____

| | |
|---|---|
| **Greatest Accomplishments** | |
| **My Biggest Impact** | |
| **Areas to Improve** | |
| **Next Steps** | |

*Weekly Affirmation*: *I am claiming success and positive energy!*

# Notes

# Weekly Reflection

Date _____ / _____ / _____

| | |
|---|---|
| **Greatest Accomplishments** | |
| **My Biggest Impact** | |
| **Areas to Improve** | |
| **Next Steps** | |

*Weekly Affirmation*: I face adversity with courage and persistence!

# Notes

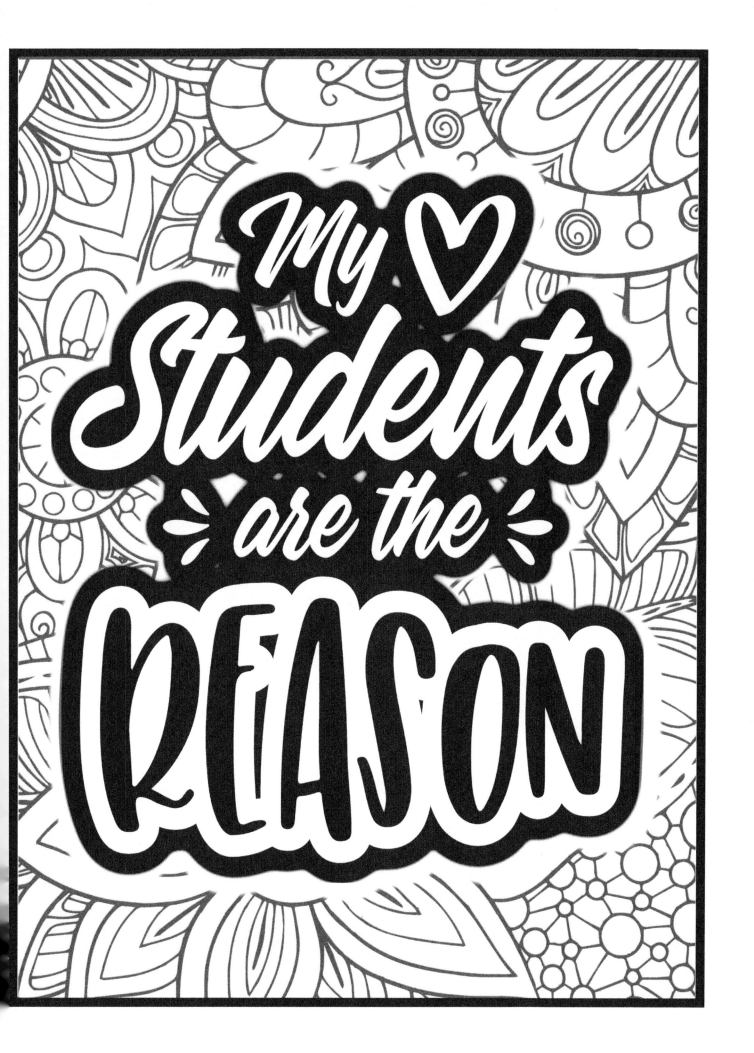

# Weekly Reflection

Date _____/_____/_____

| | |
|---|---|
| **Greatest Accomplishments** | |
| **My Biggest Impact** | |
| **Areas to Improve** | |
| **Next Steps** | |

*Weekly Affirmation:* I relinquish the need to dwell on what I can't control.

# Notes

# Weekly Reflection

Date _____/_____/_____

| | |
|---|---|
| **Greatest Accomplishments** | |
| **My Biggest Impact** | |
| **Areas to Improve** | |
| **Next Steps** | |

*Weekly Affirmation:* *I grow through what I go through!*

# Notes

Printed in Great Britain
by Amazon